Everybody likes to get a tan – it looks good and feels good. Unfortunately harsh ultra-violet radiation is now known to have an ageing effect and can even cause unsightly and life-threatening skin cancer. This simple book is full of sensible advice about how to get a cosmetically attractive tan, in summer and winter sun, with minimal risk. A regime of alternating sun and shade, careful diet and the right use of screens and unguents – all outlined here – provides the best possible protection, allowing you to enjoy your holiday to the full.

Also by Anthony Harris in Sphere Books:

THE SACRED VIRGIN AND
THE HOLY WHORE

Anthony Harris comes from Gloucestershire and
now lives in London. He attended King's College,
London, before spending two years at Trinity
College, Dublin, studying skin bacteria. He went
on to lecture for two years at Salford University
before coming to London as Senior Lecturer at the
Polytechnic of North London, teaching Human
Biochemistry to MSc postgraduates. His work on
nutrition, human performance, frame types and
fertility has been published in *Nature*, *Lancet* and
other scientific journals. As a journalist, Dr Harris
has written for the *Sun*, the *Star*, the *Daily Mirror*,
the *Daily Express*, *Vogue*, *Cosmopolitan*, *Company*,
Annabel and many other publications. He has also
written numerous popular books and text-books
which have been translated into many languages.
He is director of Anthony Harris keep-fit and
body-shaping studios, in London.

THE SAFE TAN BOOK

Anthony Harris

SPHERE BOOKS LIMITED

A SPHERE BOOK

First published in Great Britain by Sphere Books Ltd 1989
Reprinted 1989

Printed and bound in Great Britain by
Richard Clay Ltd, Bungay, Suffolk

ISBN 0 7474 0508 5

Sphere Books Ltd
A Division of
Macdonald & Co. (Publishers) Ltd
27 Wrights Lane, London W8 5TZ
A member of Maxwell Pergamon Publishing Corporation plc

The author thanks Madeleine Shaw for field testing barrier products and other tanning activities in South America, Eilat, (desert and beach), and Cyprus. Thanks to Elizabeth Arden for providing barrier creams from their range.

Contents

Author's introduction

This book is a practical and scientific guide about tanning, in other words about getting the best out of the sun.

The sun can help give you a fitter, more attractive body, strong bones and healthy teeth. It can help build up protection against minor infections and, if you are still growing, boost that growth. If you are older, it will help keep your bones strong. It is essential for the well-being of your eyes. It can beautify your skin. It cleanses impurities from your body by making you sweat healthily. It can relax you as you lie under it, and the warming rays soothe and pamper you. The sun is nature's healer of tissues, sprains and muscle aches. I could go on and on.

Most of us have enjoyed that marvellous sense of freedom on a beach as you run over the sand into the salt spray spume beneath a beaming sun. So, can anything this good ever be bad? Yes, there are risks, but they will affect most people only when the sun is abused.

By their very nature, the risks from ultraviolet

radiation can never be zero, but, just as it is impracticable to eradicate motor car accidents totally, there still exist careful and reckless driving. There is little doubt that thousands of people expose themselves to sun too abruptly, for too long, and in too intense sunlight. None of these excesses is necessary for enjoying the sun or acquiring a natural tan.

There is in fact a catch 22 situation in tanning sensibly. Your skin will not produce any pigment until it is exposed to ultraviolet radiation, but if you are excessively exposed then the pigment formation during the time of exposure cannot even begin to keep pace with the amount of radiation experienced. Result – skin damage, sunburn, skin peeling. And after that, you can't tan until the skin has healed. Clearly it is a question of balance, and in this book I have drawn together some factors, such as location, time of year, air temperature, skin types, barrier creams, length of exposure and diet to provide a guide to the way the body is perhaps happiest when being exposed to the sun. We do have defence mechanisms; they are very good, but they are not perfect, and they can be overwhelmed. As Dr Albert Kligman, M.D., Ph.D., Professor of Dermatology at the University of Pennsylvania Medical School, says, 'Every single photon (measure of light energy) reaching your skin adds, in some infinitesimal degree, to the toll of injury over the years. And this is true right across the skin colour spectrum: white, yellow, beige, brown, black. Of course, the more pigment your skin has, the more built-in protection it has. But this is still only a matter of degree – something few people realize.'

Here, then, are scientific, practical guidelines to enjoying the open air, and getting a tan without abusing two of nature's greatest resources, your body, and the sun.

Anthony Harris
London, 1989

1 · Skin deep – the anatomy of tanning

Your skin is the largest organ of your body and has many functions, some of which are improved by safe tanning, and all of which are essential to health and well-being.

It is a complex composition. For example, the skin of the scalp is specialized to produce hair, and in fact hair is part of the skin. The skin of the lips is hairless, and differs from the skin on the rest of the body; its nearest similar type is the skin of the tip of the penis and the sexual lips of the vagina. Skin is further differentiated in the formation of nails. That is why I call it an organ, for it has specific functions and is made up of differentiated tissues.

To get a clear picture of what happens in sunbathing and tanning, it is useful to have some notion of how the skin functions, and perhaps the best way to appreciate that is to consider how skin is constructed.

The first thing to be said about skin is that what you can see, the hair, the nails, the surfaces we commonly think of as skin, is all dead. It consists mainly of protein, keratin in the case of nail and hair, and flat dead cells, also mostly keratinized, on

1

the surface of the skin. The top or horny layer of the skin is constantly being worn away, sloughed off, and replaced by new cells coming up from underneath. So active is this process that, in a room with a smooth surface, say a flat mirror or a polished table top, you can see a dusty layer form there from the sloughed off skin cells of the room's inhabitants.

Technically, there are two main layers of the skin, the epidermis, and beneath that, the dermis (Figure 1a and b).

The Epidermis

The outermost layer of the epidermis consists of the protective covering of dried, dead cells that are constantly being shed and constantly replenished from the layers of growing cells beneath. It is the layer which we all see, and it can be as thick as 1 mm on the soles of the feet, or as thin as 0.1 mm on the face. It is the chief line of defence of our bodies against being swamped by water, for it is waterproof.

Beneath it is another layer, where the cells are going through the process of losing moisture and flattening, ready to take up their job of being in the front line. Beneath this layer is yet another, where the cells are still alive, not so flat, but already taking on the tough composition which will serve them, and us, well in their protective function in a world which is abrasive, and in an atmosphere which varies

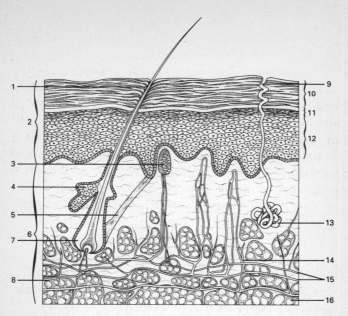

Vertical section of epidermis and dermis. Adapted from *Gray's Anatomy*.

1 Hair 2 Epidermis 3 Sense of touch organ 4 Sebaceous gland 5 Goose pimple muscle 6 Dermis 7 Hair follicle 8 Fatty tissue 9 Duct of sweat gland 10 Dead cells 11 Cells in transition 12 Zone of dividing living cells (the tanning zone) 13 Sweat gland 14 Blood supply to dermis cells 15 Blood vessels and nerves 16 Zone of elastic fibres

Cells from the dividing layer migrate out towards the surface, and die. During tanning, pigment also migrates out to colour the upper layers.

Note how the dermis dovetails into the epidermis, and how much thicker the dermis is than the outer dead layer of the epidermis.

in its radiation content, temperature and dampness.

All these cells, in their various layers, come from the underlying, germinative layer (also called the Malphigian layer) which consists of actively dividing cells, arranged several cells deep. It is here that a special kind of living cell is found, the pigment cells or, as they are technically called, the Melanocytes. It is these cells which can trap ultraviolet light and they do so by producing a pigment, melanin, brown in colour, which is ultraviolet absorptive. It is this process which actually tans the skin brown.

The Dermis

This part of the skin can be as thick as 3 mm on the back, but varies in thickness over the body from as little as 0.5 mm. It is usually thicker in men than in women, but there are great variations between people. Here are the blood vessels which nestle up against the germinative layer of the epidermis, giving nutrients to the dividing cells and taking away their waste products. Here also are the special sense cells which record heat, cold, touch, pressure and pain. The follicles or growing points of the hair fibres are also found here, and at about the same level are the sweat glands. Beneath this tough and elastic layer of living tissue is the fat layer, which can be very thick in overweight people, or just thick enough to provide a cushion for the skin upon the muscles.

The epidermis and the dermis are firmly cemented

together by a cunning piece of biological engineering: the surface of the dermis, where it meets the epidermal germinative layer, is corrugated and fibrous with elastic fibres, and this uneven surface fits exactly into corresponding dents and projections of the epidermis. The skin has its taut look in youth because the protein fibres of the dermis are tight and have a very definite pattern. They undergo some loss of elasticity and form with age, or if nutrition and exercise are faulty; a healthy blood circulation is absolutely essential to ensure nutrients are brought to the skin, and toxins taken away.

There are millions of glands in the skin. There are sweat glands which are discussed below, and associated with each hair follicle are special oil glands, the sebaceous glands, which produce an oily secretion which keeps the outermost layer of the skin supple and waterproof and can, in health, give that sheen or bloom of truly beautiful skin.

Functions of the Skin

As we've seen, there is one obvious function of the skin, and that is to prevent the wearing away of living tissue by making an outer protective layer of dead, throw-away cells. Obviously to do this well diet must feed the skin. There are many other functions too, not least of which is to make sure water is not lost in an uncontrolled manner from the living cells. If there weren't this impervious, waterpoof layer, we would all shrivel up in a very short time, and die through water loss.

Body temperature must be kept at about 36.7 to 37.2 degrees Celsius. This means that when the outside temperature falls heat must be generated, but when, as in sunbathing, the outside temperature rises heat must be lost. As soon as cold air or cold water comes into contact with the skin, the fibres contract, as do the blood vessels, so less blood circulates near the cold surface, and thereby heat loss is minimized. Extra heat is obtained by contracting the fibres of the skin. All this occurs quite automatically of course. You can see it happen because the skin blanches, losing its reddish tint in Europeans, because blood is being forced away from the surface. This process occurs in everyone; it is not so easily observable in brown or black skin, but a trained observer can spot the changes easily enough.

The other technique for keeping warmth in is to raise the hairs, thus trapping an insulating layer of air next to the skin. For most humans there is so little hair left that all you see are the bumps in the skin as the hair muscles contract. There are often no hairs sprouting at all, or those that are there are so thin and sparse it makes little difference. An echo of our hairy ancestors . . .

In contrast, the skin reddens when too much heat is being produced around it. This is not the same as sunburn; it is simply the blood vessels relaxing, becoming dilated and carrying more blood to the skin surface. This suffusion of blood is very pleasurable, and is one of the yearned-for sensations of sunbathers. It is interesting to note that just as sexual excitement involves a rush of blood to the tissues of the genitals, a blush is a sudden relaxation of the fibres in the skin, allowing blood to rush to the surface. Blushes are not always caused by embarrassment; pleasure brings a blush, so does anticipation. A good circulation then is a pleasure in itself, and as we'll learn later, there are simple techniques to improve circulation.

Does the Skin Breathe?

Most of the carbon dioxide produced by breathing is lost through the lungs, but some is given off by the skin, for it escapes from the blood vessels through the skin to the atmosphere. Some oxygen might pass through the skin into the blood, but only very little. However, a multitude of various toxic substances, most of them as yet little characterized, are lost through the pores of the skin. Sunbathing provides an ideal ambience for the skin to carry out these functions. Its importance can be judged by the wonderful rejuvenating feeling sunbathing gives. The bad smells of over-clothed and confined bodies give ample evidence to suggest that the skin should be allowed to have its day, as it were, free of encumbrances, basking in the warmth, being soothed but not baked.

Society and Your Skin

Skin is what you see of a person, and it is little wonder therefore that we spend so much time and money on it. It can be coloured in different ways by cosmetics, the hair dressed, nails pedicured and manicured, and the surface adorned by jewels and clothes; all the age-old techniques of attraction are brought to bear on the skin.

But its visual aspect is not the only one; there is the texture of it, and the smell of it. Tanning can improve the texture, but taken too far it ruins it. A healthy texture depends on the proper degree of exposure, a good diet, and not being overweight. As for the smell of the body, well, as we've seen, sunbathing is a sure way of improving that – provided you let the body function as it was meant to. All these factors come together in sunbathing, and so have to be combined to achieve that beautiful, vibrant, tanned look.

2 · How to protect your skin in the sun

There are two main responses of the skin to sunlight. One is an increase of the superficial layers, which toughens the skin; the other is an increase in pigmentation leading to a deepening of the brownness of the skin.

These changes occur because, although sunlight is of great importance to health, particularly in producing the bone forming vitamin D in an active form in the skin, too much heat or too much ultraviolet radiation can damage cells.

The thickening of the skin involves an acceleration in the production of the outermost layer of the epidermis, the cells which are toughened with keratin protein. The increase of pigment in the skin, however, is rather more complicated.

The Chemical Factory

In the lower layers of the epidermis are the melanocytes, which produce pigment called melanin, using protein materials to do so. The process is triggered to a greater degree of activity when ultraviolet rays penetrate the outer, dead layer and are absorbed by the living cells of the epidermis. The chemical factory is then set in motion and the melanocytes produce the brown pigment. The result is a darkening of the skin, and this occurs whether the skin is brown, black, white or yellow.

There are twig-like processes coming out of the melanocytes, and these extend into the layers of dying cells which are destined to become the scaly protective layer forming the surface of the skin. So the process of tanning occurs inside the skin, and the chemical products are then taken up to the surface with the scaly cells. As you tan you are actually making pigment to reinforce the keratin of the skin as a barrier against excessive bombardment of living cells beneath by radiation or heat.

Colour of Skin

Actually the skin colour, though it can be changed by tanning, depends on other pigments too. Blood in the dermis will be blue in the veins and red in the arteries, and you can see these forms of the blood pigment, haemoglobin, in various parts of the body. The pink of the mucous membranes like the lips, and the tip of the penis, or the lips of the vagina is mostly from the oxygenated form of the blood pigment. However, they can turn blue, especially in the cold, because then the blood supply is sluggish and the bluish colour of the veins predominates. Other pigments are the yellow carotenes, involved in vitamin A production, and another brownish pigment, melanoid, which is diffusely located throughout the epidermis.

The number of melanocytes in human skin is about a thousand in an area of a pinhead, varying over parts of the body, with greater concentrations in such areas as the areola surrounding the nipples. They also vary in number from individual to individual, but the number is the same on average in people with brown skin or fair skin. What is different, however, is that people who are ethnically brown produce more melanin from the same amount of cells and the same amount of sunlight. The pituitary gland controls, through a secretion called MSH (melanin stimulating hormone), the rate at which melanin is made by the pigment cells.

Here are the actual phases of change in the tanning process:

1. On the first exposure to sun, the melanin already present actually darkens.
2. If continued exposure occurs, the melanocytes make more melanin.
3. If the exposure is continued over a longer period, say months, then the number of active pigment cells is increased.

If the tanning process is stopped, its permanence will depend on what stage has been reached in the above phases.

Along with these colour changes occur the thickening and toughening processes of the skin mentioned earlier. Obviously, tanning is a major change in the human body, and consequently there's a bonus in understanding what is happening so it can be done safely and with the greatest benefit. What, then, are the common hazards and how may they be best dealt with, so that eventually a tanning method is achieved that is safe, pleasurable and cosmetically acceptable? We'll look first at the most common problem, sunburn.

Sunburn

When the skin is exposed too long to the sun's ultraviolet rays, the defence mechanism of tanning cannot cope and blistering of the skin occurs. This is sunburn, and it results in an increase of fluid in the skin as blood vessels weep plasma into the connective skin tissue. The outer layer breaks down, the skin peels and blisters may form. The skin reddens because the blood supply is accelerated to take away breakdown products and also to reduce the temperature of the skin.

These effects can be avoided by gradual exposure to the sun, and that depends entirely on the history of your skin during the preceding few months. If you live in Britain or Europe, then relatively little ultraviolet light reaches most of your body; so if you go out into the tropical sun and lie in it for anything more than a few minutes in the first exposure, you can get a burn, with itching and stinging sensations to go along with it. However, sudden exposure to the reflected light from snow, as on skiing holidays, can also result in sunburn, even though you are not aware of any heat. This emphasizes the main point: the destruction of skin tissue occurs primarily from ultraviolet rays in the sunlight, not from heat.

If you have been in the habit of being out of doors, with some measure of your body exposed to dilute European sun, then you will be partially tanned anyway, and so when you lie in more intense sunlight your skin is already pre-conditioned. Today, of course, you can use ultraviolet sun beds, and pre-condition the skin indoors. Fortunately, reputable beauty salons and manufacturers of these tanning aids give strict instructions for their use. Careless use can be harmful but gradual exposure is merely a matter of strictly following the laid-down procedure. It is the enticement of beach and sea which can lead to over-exposure.

Exposure Procedures

You can train your body by frequent exposure to dilute sunshine, keeping exposure to hot sun to short intervals, say less than half an hour a day at first, until the tan begins to develop. After a couple of days, periods of exposure can be gradually leng-thened day by day. However, it must be emphasized that, since the breasts, back and thighs, as well as the buttocks, are not usually exposed to the sun in most parts of the world, the sudden donning of a bikini, or less, exposes areas of skin which may have no protection against the sun at all. Gently does it, with short duration exposure, building up to longer tanning times, and special care given to the more vulnerable parts of the body (figure 2).

Being Active in the Sun

It is stationary exposure, without preparation, for a lengthy amount of time, which is the danger. Even running about without protection, playing beach ball, for the same amount of time as lying directly in the sun is much, much less hazardous. If you are active in the sun the exposure on one place is very much reduced, since for at least half the time any part of your body will be facing away from the sun and for a good deal of the rest of the time will be obliquely placed to the sun's rays. In short, the exposure, say for the test site in the middle of your back, might be only ten per cent as compared with the hundred per cent lying prone and stationary in the sun's direct rays.

By the way, you get a beautiful, all-over tan by playing games out in the sun, and the reason is that the constant movement of the body into different positions relative to the sun exposes all parts in some degree to the sun's rays. Also, when you are

14

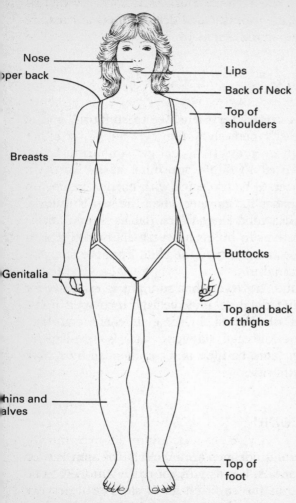

Nose

Upper back

Lips

Back of Neck

Top of shoulders

Breasts

Genitalia

Buttocks

Top and back of thighs

Shins and calves

Top of foot

Areas especially at risk of sunburn.

15

active, the blood supply to the skin is improved. This means all the sophisticated defence mechanisms are at their maximum efficiency.

Toddlers

Children's skin is very sensitive to sunburn, and of course, left to themselves, they will happily scamper about with no protection, and get sunburnt. Active children, used to dilute sunshine, as in Northern Europe, need to be protected with barrier creams on sunny beaches in Summer when the sun is intense. Sun hats are good for toddlers. Babies should not be left out in the sun unless it is very diffuse. If the skin starts to redden, remove the child from the sun and give it a cool drink.

Remember however that sunlight is essential for growth and children may be left uncovered if the sun is diffuse. Indeed, in some northern countries where the average daylight sun is insufficient, ultraviolet lamp bathing is recommended by school health authorities.

Old People

The general guidelines are precisely the same as for younger adults, but as you get older you tend to be less active in the sun and go to sleep or doze very easily. Take care then that you do not fall asleep under intense sun without protection, from shade, barrier creams, and suitable clothing.

Pregnancy

Sunshine is important because it helps a pregnant woman provide vitamin D for herself and her baby, and also because of the soothing effects of the sun's infra-red rays. However, pregnancy is a time of considerable stress on the body's fluid regulation mechanism and, as we've seen, too much heat can upset the balance.

Sunbathing for pregnant women is useful, but excessive exposure, without adequate clothes or barrier protection, is not recommended.

Treatment of Sunburn

If you have reddening of the skin, itching and tingling, then you are probably sunburned. In severe cases a fever develops. You need to keep out of the sun until these symptoms stop. The discomfort can be reduced by various skin lotions and creams, such as calamine lotion, though there are many other brands now available. Whichever lotions and creams you use is a matter of personal preference, though any good pharmacist can supply dozens of brands, all equally effective.

Barrier Creams and Tanning

Ultraviolet rays cannot damage cells unless they pass into them, so if creams or lotions which absorb these rays are applied to the skin the cells are protected in direct proportion to the absorbing power of the chemicals inside the application. Today there are dozens of different materials used and, by using different blends of ingredients, cosmetic chemists have achieved a whole range of products designed to give as little or great absorption of ultraviolet rays as required. On the practical level, it can mean you are free to expose skin to the sun without running the risk of sunburn. However, if the barrier factor is very high and the sunshine relatively weak, no tanning will occur. You can select the barrier level you want, erring on the side of caution, and apply the preparation over all the parts of your body which you are going to expose, remembering lips and nipples.

Because most of the barrier creams are oil based, they do not wash away appreciably in sea water or by sweating. They can however be removed at night by washing all over with soap and water.

Products for Protection

Leading cosmetic companies formulate skin protection creams and gels to absorb ultraviolet radiation selectively. Such products are given a number to indicate their efficiency in screening this radiation from the skin. They are variously called barrier creams, sunscreens, and so forth. The highest factor in standard, recognized ranges is 34, that is the Sun Protection Factor (SPF) is 34. Other products in their ranges are less absorptive. All reputable companies test their products for allergy reaction, and incorporate the best medicinal expertise in their formulations. Be sure to read the product label carefully, and only purchase from a reputable chemist, druggist, apothecary or drugstore which will have a qualified pharmacist to advise you on the product you wish to purchase. Today you can enjoy the open air without harming your skin, by protecting it with a range of products. Below I give the kind of product to use.

Superblock Cream – SPF 34

This is designed to give the skin maximum protection against the sun and help prevent premature ageing. With proper application, this cream provides all-day protection against painful and dangerous burning with the highest protection sunblock. It protects at SPF 34 while sunning and still provides SPF 24 protection after eighty minutes in the water. Its emollient-rich moisturizers help keep skin soft and supple. It can be used for children and infants over six months of age. Care must be taken when returning to locations of dilute sunshine not to use these barriers on children because vitamin D (which is produced in the skin by sunshine) is essential to them for growth. Apply generously and evenly. Massage in, concentrating on burn-prone areas – lips, nose, under-eyes, ears, shoulders and the backs of knees. Apply thirty minutes before sun exposure and re-apply after eighty minutes in the water.

Oil-Free Ultra Block – SPF 15

This clear fluid gel lets you get a minimal healthy-looking tan while giving soothing, greaseless sun-burn protection. Use it if you want an invisible sunscreen that leaves no oily film. Oil-Free Ultra Block will give 15 times your natural protection against sunburn. It can be worn over a moisturizer for added sun protection.

Spot Protection Sunblock – SPF 15

This solid stick product gives spot protection for ultra-sensitive areas – lips, eyelids, nose, toes and tops of ears. It protects, moisturizes and conditions the skin. Apply before sun exposure and re-apply after swimming or exercise. Designed for year-round use. Very useful for sports enthusiasts.

Sun Shading Cream – SPF 8

Sun Shading Cream is a water-resistant formula that fulfils the fair or delicate skin's need for both moisture and major sunscreen protection. It helps prevent painful sunburn even in high-risk situations such as skiing, on the beach or at high altitudes. This cream is designed for skin that often burns before tanning so it is useful for fair and redheaded people. It retains its full protection even after forty minutes of swimming or vigorous exercise. It allows for a measured, gradual tan. However, never overdo exposure.

Oil-Free Tanning Gel – SPF 6

This clear, fluid gel offers invisible, greaseless sunburn protection whilst allowing a healthy-looking tan to develop. It is suitable for moderate sun.

Sun Tanning Cream – SPF 4

A moisture-rich cream for medium sunburn protection, it encourages a rich, golden tan. Smooth in to supplement the skin's own natural supply of moisture – it even helps protect against the damaging effects of wind and weather. It lets you stay in the sun four times longer without burning than with no protection.

Dark Tanning Gel – SPF 2

A light protection emollient gel for deep, fast tanning, this is for serious sunbathers who tan easily and rarely burn and for those who are already protected by a tan. Untanned fair skin will have sunburn protection for up to thirty minutes, medium skin for forty minutes and for dark skin fifty minutes. It is suitable for weak but warm sun.

Fast Bronzing Oil

For sun-worshippers who are already protected by a tan, this lightly tinted oil encourages fast, deep bronzing and helps maintain your skin's own moisture level and softness. It has no sun protection factor. It is essential that bronzing preparations are never confused with SPF products. Use only in moderate sun and with limited exposure.

Self-Tanning Lotion

Use for the look of a healthy tan without going into the sun. Within hours it gives skin the look of a tan that will last for several days without sun or dyes. Use it all over or to fill in strap marks and areas the sun has missed. Creamy Self-Tanning Lotion moisturizes as it 'tans'. It can be used in conjunction with sunscreens. Apply Self-Tanning Lotion first and allow to dry. Then use a sunscreen as directed before sun exposure. A Self-Tanning Lotion 'tan' is not a true tan and therefore provides no protection against ultraviolet radiation. Different products vary in their coloration. You may find one to your taste.

After Sun Moisture Refresher

This contains special emollients to cool, smooth and moisturize skin. It helps prevent flaking, peeling and dryness, and enhances a healthy tan. It does not contain a sunscreen.

3 · Exposure guide

Although naturally black skin can withstand more exposure than very fair, white skin, the fact remains that lying immobile in tropical sun, even when it isn't at its brightest and most powerful at noon, is not recommended for any kind of skin. There is just too much ultraviolet radiation present. Accordingly, it is a simple historical and social fact that all people who have lived in areas of the world where the sun is bright and hot have over the centuries developed methods of covering their bodies, heads and faces, often leaving only the eyes bare, but protected by the brim of a hat, turban or typical Arab head-dress. It is only during the last few decades that cheap travel has meant that millions of Europeans, with fair skin, can suddenly transport themselves from dilute north European sun into the Mediterranean or even the Tropics. The result has been a great increase in the number of people suffering sunburn, heat stroke, and risking progressive changes in their skin, not the least of which is an increase in the ageing effect which even dilute sunshine produces.

Skin Types

The fairer you are, the longer it takes to tan, but even if you have black skin, you will get blacker skin if you move from Europe to a hotter clime.

Fair, white skin, often associated with very pale blond hair and blue eyes, will tan, but the process is lengthy and certainly shouldn't be attempted in a few days, or even weeks. People with celtic colouring, red hair, white skin, green or blue eyes, are perhaps the most sensitive of all, and sometimes do not tan evenly; the face, for example, becomes freckled. Freckles are really small and localized tanning areas. Another kind of skin which is very vulnerable to the sun is that of the dark-haired, green-eyed person, whose skin is not so much fair, but white on unexposed areas.

Mediterranean and Arabic colouring, namely brown skin, black hair and brown eyes, will take a tan quicker because the pigment production cells respond more quickly to the ultraviolet radiation, and in any case there is already pigment in the skin. Indians also fall into this category and it is noticeable that children of Asian parents born, say, in Bradford or Southall, England, often have complexions as light as Greeks.

Chinese and Japanese colouring will respond to a tan, but at a rate no faster than Arabs, in fact a little slower in most cases.

Blacks have the largest amount of pigment, but exposure will intensify the blackness. White skin can never become as tanned as black skin by sun alone, although there is a disease condition in which hormonal change can lead to blackening of the white and brown skin when exposed to sunlight.

Maintaining a Tan

All skins lose tan when exposure to the sun's rays is reduced. It can take days, or weeks, depending on the extent of the tan, but this means a permanent tan requires repeated exposure to the sun. Common sense suggests that one has to balance the desire for a tan against the needs of your body to recuperate from ultraviolet radiation. Excessive tanning is when, for example, North European women develop a near mahogany colour by really severe exposure to Mediterranean sun. However, provided the level of tanning desired is not excessive, there is something to be said for maintaining a reasonable tan. If for instance you work out of doors, like many labourers do, and regularly expose your arms, you find that even in dilute European sun, white skin will develop a tan. This is probably the safest kind of tanning, achieved through very low dosage of sun radiation and being active in the sun.

Air Temperature and Exposure

In general the more intense the sun, the greater the temperature of the air, but you can be misled by breeze, or diffuse cloud, into thinking the intensity of the sun is less than it is because it doesn't feel very hot. This is particularly true on a beach with a sea breeze, or on a ski slope. However, the sun may be very intense indeed. As a rule of thumb, high temperatures during daylight mean that high ultraviolet radiation will be falling on your skin, but the reverse is not always the case.

In the tropics air temperature can near 30°C (86°F) much of the year while a comfortable room temperature in Europe is about 18°C. If the humidity is high even 25°C feels hot, but when the air is dry with a breeze (bringing the temperature down) the body feels more comfortable; however beware of mistaking this as a sign that the sun is less intense. The breeze does not blow away radiation!

Exposure Around the World

It is very instructive to realize just how different the sun is in different parts of the world. The degree of difference in its intensity is astonishing, and people used to European sun, diluted by cloud, moisture and the low angle (which has the effect of spreading the sun's rays out over a larger area, and so diminishing their intensity) are often totally un-prepared for noonday Mediterranean sun, and very ill-equipped to meet tropical sun, several hours either side of noon, even for doses of just fifteen minutes.

When the temperature is about 19–20 degrees

Celsius, exposure should be kept to within half an hour a day and, depending on your skin type, barrier creams should be used. Above 21°C, say to 26°C, exposure should be even less, or the highest factor barrier cream should be used. Above 26°C means intense exposure to ultraviolet rays and unless the skin is already well tanned even a few minutes' exposure on sensitive parts of the body, like the nipples, may be too high.

It should be understood that a few minutes' exposure to tropical sun at noon is much more damaging to unprotected skin than many hours of dilute autumn sun in Europe. This is because the intense sun on untanned skin immediately over-whelms the skin's defences; *until some melanin is produced, the skin is entirely defenceless.* As soon as some, preferably moderate, sunlight has been experienced by the skin, pigment is produced and will be available for tanning and defence of the skin within a few days. Once this has happened you can enjoy the sun. However, always protect continuously – it is better to use too high a filter factor in your barrier cream and not get tanned at all at first, rather than over-expose.

Countries and Locations of Intense Sun

Countries and seas within 15° latitude North or South of the Equator have very intense sun for many hours during the day and for most of the year. *Extreme caution* is required when exposing unprotected skin to such sun. If there is sand, the effect is heightened. Altitude too increases sunburning radiation, as does snow.

The countries in these regions are:

Equator
Central Africa, N Congo, Cameroons, Northern Brazil, S Venezuela, Ecuador, Southern Colombia, South East Indies.

Within 15° of the Equator
North
Somaliland, Sahara Desert, Guinea, Panama, Philippines, Sri Lanka, S India
South
Southern Congo, Central Brazil, N Bolivia and N Peru, N Australia

Between 15 and 35° Latitude, North and South
Here there are also many hours of intense sun each day for much of the year, although for two hours before sunset and two hours after sunrise the intensity is much less than in the countries listed above. There is also greater variation between winter and summer than in the tropics. For Northern climes, winter occurs in the later months and early part of the year; in Southern climes these are the summer months.

The countries in these regions are:
North
Egypt, N Philippines, S Mexico, S India, Vietnam,

Red Sea, Tripoli, Tunis, Morocco, S States of the
USA, S Japan, S China, N India, Iran, Israel,
Countries of the Southern Mediterranean

South

N Australia, South Africa, S Peru, Bolivia, S
Brazil, Paraguay, Uruguay, N Argentina, Central
Australia

Locations with well-defined Winter and Summer, with many hours each day of intense sun in the Summer

These countries are found between latitudes 35° and
45°, North and South. The advantage of these
countries to the sunbather is that if you gradually
expose your body in the cooler months you tan very
naturally, so when the hot sun comes your body is
protected. Nonetheless, the summer sun is still to be
treated with caution.

The countries in these regions are:

North

S France, Spain, Portugal, Central USA, Central
Japan, Central China, Caspian and Black Sea,
North Mediterranean, Turkey, Greece, Italy

South

Central Argentina, S Australia, New Zealand

Countries and Locations of dilute sun for most of the year

These are found between latitudes 40° and 55°,

North and South. Summer sun is only available for a few hours each day and for only about three months, but can be intense at noon. The winters can be bitter, with very little sun, so that sudden exposure to summer sun can be hazardous for people living in these regions.

The countries in these regions are:

North
  Britain excluding Scotland, N France, Northern States of the USA, S Canada, N Japan, N China, S Russia, Germany

South
  S Argentina

Countries and Locations of Little Sun

Beyond 55° latitude
Here there is sun for a few hours a day for only a month or so. Thereafter even visibility falls in the Winter.

The countries in this region are:
Scotland, Alaska, Central Russia, Scandinavia, Denmark, Iceland.

Beyond 65° latitude
Here Arctic and Antarctic conditions are encountered: darkness for most hours for a large part of the year, with almost permanent snow. However, the Summers can be very hot, though of short duration.

A useful guide to the sun's power of radiation is as follows:

Intense Sun	Sun at noon, in a cloud-less sky (Tropics) *Expose skin with greatest caution*
Moderate to Strong Sun	Sun two hours either side of noon in a clear or hazy cloud sky *Expose skin with caution*
Dilute Sun	Sun three or more hours before or after noon, with hazy cloud *Exposure determined by comfort*

Remember, exposure = Strength of Sun multiplied by Duration of Exposure

Aide Memoire of Sensible Exposure to the Sun

Sunbathing

1. Change position often in even moderate sun.
2. Use appropriate barrier cream.
3. Use good sunglasses.
4. Make sure lips and nipples are well protected with barrier cream.
5. Take special care you do not sunburn genitals (use clothing or cream, or both).

6. Limit exposure on first day to 20–25 minutes in moderate sun, while for intense sun expose for even less time, with ample barrier cream application. This is particularly important to light-skinned people.
7. Never expose to intense sun until you have a tan, even with barrier cream.
8. Remember early morning sun and late evening sun is much less intense, start off sunbathing at these times. Noonday sun even in Southern Europe can be *intense*.
9. Second day, same as first.
10. When tan begins to develop, after two to four days, filter factor of barrier can be reduced from maximum to medium range.

Playing in the Sun: On Beaches

1. Remember shoulders are constantly exposed.
2. Remember sweat may reduce efficiency of barrier cream.
3. Sea breezes may delude you into thinking that the sun is less strong than it really is.

Playing in the Sun: In Boats

The soft lulling of the movement of water can cause you to fall asleep. This and the reflection of light from the water can lead to over-exposure. Take extra care and protect with cream or clothing.

At Altitude

Just because there is snow, this does not mean the sun is not intense; there may not be enough sun for long enough to melt millions of tons of snow, but quite enough to burn your skin. Use barrier creams for exposed parts.

The Strength of the Sun and Tanning

Sunburn-producing rays will not pass through glass, but will pass through the skin and cause pigment reaction. However, smog, smoke and thick cloud will absorb most of the rays. None the less, light cloud still allows most of the rays through, and you can be led astray by exposing yourself too long in such conditions, as sunburn can result. The factors to watch for are water, snow and sand, since reflection increases the sunburning power of the rays already coming directly on to you.

Altitude is an important factor because, although the air on mountains may be cool, an effect even more apparent when there is a wind, the atmosphere is thinner, and you are often above urban pollution; so the sun may be as much as twenty times as strong as in the valleys. If there is snow, the effect is increased yet more. Paradoxically, you can get sunburned very easily on a skiing holiday surrounded by snow. Protect your face with barrier creams, and use a moisturizer just before going to bed.

The power of the tropical sun arises from several factors, such as the absence of industrial pollution. The sun's direct arc overhead means that there is less of the spreading effect mentioned earlier; it is virtually absent at noon, the rays pouring straight down with great intensity. The lower the sun is, the more atmosphere it has to pass through, so in temperate climes, even in summer, much of the ultraviolet is filtered out before about 10 am and after 4 pm. This effect occurs in the tropics, but is much less marked.

It should be remembered that, though many screen preparations are adhesive to the skin, it is wise to apply the preparation about half an hour before exposure to the sun. Also, although they are oil-based, and therefore resistant to the effects of sweat, some is inevitably lost as you turn over on the sun mat, or whatever else your skin comes into contact with. Hence, the barrier creams should be applied more than once during sunbathing. Obviously if you swim you should then apply more barrier cream afterwards.

It is absolutely essential to remember that if you have become sunburnt, and your skin peels, you have hardly any protection against the risks of ultraviolet exposure, and you should keep out of the sun. Also, when the skin is burnt, it becomes vulnerable to bacteria and fungal spores, which can lead to infection.

Perhaps the safest time to sunbathe is when it is just that little bit too cold to lie out with only a bathing costume, or less on. In these conditions you have to be active, and the kind of tanning that is achieved in dilute sun, combined with action, produces the most durable and deep tan, with the least ageing and also the best cosmetic effect. It really gives that tawny, outdoor look, which is noticeably absent in the tan of people who bake themselves by sudden exposure to midday sun.

This advice is something fair-skinned people might note, since some of them, especially redheads, may never truly tan, as their melanocytes are rather sluggish. However, by being active in sports in moderate sunshine, not risking sunburn, it will soon become apparent over a period of weeks if you are going to tan. Usually you will, and it will be most attractive, the healthy response to healthy environmental conditions. Severe sun is not a healthy environmental situation for your naked, unprepared human skin.

4 · Fat and tanning

As we've seen, tanning is a two-fold process, involving the pigmentation of the skin, and the increase in skin thickness, as adaptive processes to exposure to ultraviolet and heat rays from the sun or from special lamps. In one sense this is independent of the amount of fat in the body, but a good supply of blood and nutrients is essential for the skin to be healthy, and the fact is that too much fat does interfere with the amount of blood which can reach the living skin. It is a matter of common observation that the tightly stretched skin of the overweight does not tan so quickly or so well as skin which is not carrying the burden of too much fat.

Here is a simple guide to seeing how much overweight you are. You are definitely carrying too much fat beneath the skin if:

a) you can pinch out more than 2 to 3 cm next to your navel when you are standing up
b) pinch out more than 2 cm on your inner thigh near the crotch.

Of course there are other standards too, but these

have the value of immediacy and simplicity; you can do the test any time you like.

If you do have this problem, use slimming diets, massage, and exercise. Remember, you don't have to crash diet, as this will ruin your skin; it will become wrinkled and sagging before its time.

Tanning Weight

As you can see from table 1, if you are slim, you have less surface area to tan, but if you plump up to a heavier weight your area exposed to the sun gets larger. The problem with this is quite simply that you have no greater number of pigment forming cells, so your skin is more vulnerable now it is stretched out. That is why the ideal weight for your frame size can be called your tanning weight.

Table 1: Tanning Area and Body Weight

Height	Weight	Skin Area
5'6" (165 cms)	110 pounds (50 kg): slim	1.5 sq. metres
	140 pounds (64 kg)	1.7 sq. metres
5'10" (178 cms)	140 pounds (64 kg): slim	1.8 sq. metres
	170 pounds (77 kg)	1.95 sq. metres

Table 2, which I have used for many years, gives the tanning weights for men and women; it provides a good guide. Use it in conjunction with the pinch test. You can remove excess weight using slimming diets, but the main thing is to get to a good weight and keep it. The problem with yo-yoing in weight is that the skin will sooner or later be stretched beyond its elasticity, and you will end up with loose,

Table 2: Tanning Weights

Healthy weights for men (in pounds):

Height	Wiry	Average	Large
5ft	103	119	131
5ft 1in	106	122	134
5ft 2in	108	126	137
5ft 3in	112	129	141
5ft 4in	115	132	145
5ft 5in	118	136	149
5ft 6in	121	139	153
5ft 7in	125	144	158
5ft 8in	129	148	162
5ft 9in	133	152	166
5ft 10in	137	157	171
5ft 11in	140	161	175
6ft	144	166	180
6ft 1in	148	171	185
6ft 2in	153	176	190
6ft 3in	158	181	195
6ft 4in	163	186	200
6ft 5in	168	191	205

Healthy weights for women (in pounds):

Height	Small	Average	Large
5ft	100	108	123
5ft 1in	103	111	126
5ft 2in	106	114	129
5ft 3in	109	118	133
5ft 4in	112	122	137
5ft 5in	116	126	141
5ft 6in	120	130	145
5ft 7in	124	134	149
5ft 8in	128	138	154
5ft 9in	132	142	159
5ft 10in	136	146	164
5ft 11in	140	150	169

Adapted from *Overdrive*, Dr A B Harris

haggard looking skin, which will not be healthy, and will not tan well.

The weights shown in the tables are for fully grown men and women of twenty-five years, measured without shoes and weighed nude. Unless you are of exceptional skeletal and muscular build you can't weigh more than the weights in the last column without being grossly overweight.

Frame size is first identified by skeletal dimensions, since the wider, deeper, thicker your bones are, the greater the possible muscular development. The following gives a guide for assessing your category (measure the joints at their thinnest part):

Men

Frames	Wiry	Average	Large
Wrist	less than 6½in	6½–7in	above 7in
Ankle	less than 8¼in	8¼–9in	above 9in

Women

Frames	Small	Average	Large
Wrist	less than 5¾in	5¾–6¼in	above 6¼in
Ankle	less than 8in	8–8¾in	above 8¾in

If you have broad shoulders and a deep chest with truly large bone joints you go into the large category. The wiry build is narrow in width and depth.

Check your weight in the charts. Women should be about 6lb and men about 10lb inside the weights given for health for your frame type. If you are outside the limits, you need to lose weight. Remember, if you are overweight at twenty-five, then forty-five may see you very, very large indeed. Keeping slim is perhaps the golden rule of health and looks.

Cells and Circulation

Of the billions of cells making up your body, every one must get some oxygen, and the only way it can get it is from the blood. This is pumped to every part of the body, carrying oxygen from the lungs, obtained from the air we breathe. Cells which do not get sufficient oxygen cannot carry on, while the waste they make stockpiles instead of passing back into the blood. The circulation of blood carries waste protein from the cells of the skin and other tissues first to the liver, where it is converted to urea, and then to the kidneys, where it is filtered out to be expelled from the body in the urine.

We can now begin to see how important exercise is, because exercise keeps the heart, which pumps blood, healthy and makes sure blood passes through our tissues.

But blood is also a communication network, carrying chemicals, known as hormones, which regulate the functions of different parts of the body and allow them to work together in a co-ordinated way. There are a large number of hormones and they are made by many glands in different parts of the body. Hormones usually have their effect some distance away from where they are made. The pituitary gland, for instance, is located within the brain and hormones from this gland regulate growth of muscles and bones, the reproductive cycle and also the production of melanin in the skin.

Cellulite

Cellulite results in a puckered appearance of the skin, usually at the tops of legs. It can appear as often on slim girls as muscular or plump ones. It is, however, seldom found in men since an additional factor aggravating the condition is female hormonal imbalance. Basically the fat beneath the skin, instead of being smooth, is in stripes, or even nodules. Here the circulation is very poor, so cellulite areas will not tan well.

It happens because of:

a) Lack of exercise
b) Too much fat in the diet.
c) Crash-dieting, and hormonal imbalance.

To prevent it, cut down on animal fats. Swimming, particularly the crawl and breast-stroke alternately, is super for the upper legs, and prevents cellulite. Massage yourself regularly.

5 · Real skin food

Every part of the body and skin requires food, which is made up of nutrients. A nutrient is food which can be absorbed into your bloodstream. It is then taken around the body to where it has a definite function to perform; digested proteins, for example, are used to make the outer layer of your skin.

Without nutrients, the living process at first functions poorly, then comes to a halt. What are the nutrients? They are carbohydrates, proteins, fats, vitamins and minerals; each of these has important roles to play in keeping skin healthy so that it tans well. However, we know today that in order to get the best out of good food you have to help the digestive process by stimulating the intestinal tract with fibre, so, although it is not strictly a nutrient, it acts as an accessory to *real skin food*.

Proteins

Proteins are made of chains of simpler units, called amino acids. Every protein has a number of these;

there are over twenty common amino acids. You digest protein in your stomach and intestine, breaking it down into its constituent amino acids, which then pass into your bloodstream. Eventually they are used to make your own proteins, skin, muscles, hair etc. Good sources of proteins are cereals, milk, cheese, fish, meat, eggs, beans and nuts.

Carbohydrates

These are the starches and sugars, and they are our chief energy source. Sugars come in various forms. Sucrose, for instance, is our ordinary cane sugar, fructose is found in fruit, maltose comes from starch, galactose is found in milk. All of these, however, are converted to glucose during digestion. Reserves of glucose are stored in the liver, part of whose function is to control the amount of sugar in the blood. Good sources of carbohydrates are cereals and fruits.

Fats

It may seem strange to hear that fat is important, but without it your skin will not be tough and elastic. Smooth skin, good body contours, even your brain and nervous system depend on fat. But how can that be true, when all we hear about fat is that it is bad for you? The answer lies in choosing good not bad fats in your diet.

45

The fats you find in plant oils, nuts, the skins of fruits and vegetables – minute amounts, but of the highest quality – and in liver and fish, are very good. These are unsaturated fats. Cheese, butter and, to a lesser extent, yoghurt also contribute to the wide mix of fats we must have. A diet rich in animal fats tends to produce harder fat layers under the skin than you would obtain by eating a more balanced fat diet. Excessive fat intake of any kind is unhealthy. The aim is to have a widely chosen, fresh, diet. Consequently plant produce, which contains the unsaturated fats, must figure in a good diet, but so must dairy produce and meat. Cellulite is a rumpled fat layer. It is extremely common in women, whose animal fat intake corresponds to nearly half their calorie intake.

Oils are easily absorbed through the skin, and in Mediterranean countries it has been a centuries-old practice to rub olive oil into the skin. In the cases where cellulite has been caught early enough, a smoother contour has resulted from this treatment. Lecithins, which are found in concentrated form in yolks of eggs, liver and brains, are used by cosmetic manufacturers too for skin moisturizers.

Fibre

When you eat whole grain cereals there is always a large amount of indigestible residue, called fibre. After digestion of grain in the stomach and small intestine, the fibre passes into the large intestine, and helps to keep it in good tone. Fibre can be obtained from vegetables, fruit, nuts, bran, wholemeal breakfast cereals and wholemeal bread.

The latest research shows that fibre enables your digestive system actually to get more out of your food and put it into your tissues.

Vitamins

Your good looks and vitality for now and the future depend on tiny amounts of special figure-forming, zest-making, materials in your food. They are called vitamins.

Vitamin A

This vitamin is formed from the digestion of carotene, found in carrots, tomatoes, and many other red and orange coloured vegetables. It also occurs in fish oils, butter and meat – particularly liver. It is needed for a healthy skin. Vitamin A actually makes your eyes shine, as well as keeping them healthy. It is also essential for healthy skin – a deficiency will cause it to become rough, dry and blotchy.

Vitamin D

This is found in milk, cheese and fish. Our most important day-to-day source, however, is sunshine which promotes the manufacture of vitamin D in the skin. Vitamin D is essential for the absorption of calcium and the formation of bone. A deficiency of it can cause the disease rickets which was, in the past, common in children growing up in cities, in areas of poor sunlight. Cod liver oil is a sure remedy for rickets, but the best and most natural way of getting enough vitamin D is regular and sensible exposure to sunlight.

Vitamin E

Widely distributed in foods, especially in wholemeal bread, wheat germ and wheat germ oil, this vitamin promotes normal growth, development, general vigour, good circulation and the health of body cells.

Vitamin C

Research has shown that low levels of vitamin C mean lassitude, fatigue, tiredness and even deep fits of the blues. This vitamin has very far-reaching effects and is important to the whole body, including the skin. Without it, you'll lose zest and become vulnerable to disease. With it, you'll be really vital. It is essential to the production of collagen, the connective tissue of the cells, which helps towards the suppleness and firmness of the skin. You can get the basic amount in a fresh orange every day, but if you have salads, vegetables and other fruit, you can boost your daily intake to five or six times the minimum, so taking care of your skin very well.

The B Vitamins

Often called the B complex, there are several different B vitamins. They are usually found in the same foods (particularly wheat germ, liver, cheese and eggs), but they all have precise and different functions. They all, however, contribute to general health and recent findings point to their importance in mental health and the ability of the body to cope with stress. The following are of particular importance to the skin:

Thiamin B1

This is the energy giver, it helps the vital processes in each and every cell where energy is released from food to power your everyday actions.

Riboflavin B2

This is probably the most important skin vitamin. The effects of not getting enough are unpleasant, and include dermatotis, eczema, cracked lips and mouth ulcers. Good skin needs vitamin B2 to remain in an attractive condition.

Niacin B3

Another skin vitamin, but also an energy booster.

Pantothenic acid B5

Essential for the correct usage of fats, and so a must in all reducing diets. It helps the body burn up excess fatty tissue. Yet another vitamin for the skin, it guards against too dry a texture, and may slow the ageing process. It is widely found in many foods, including lean steak, yeast extract, eggs.

Pyridoxine, Vitamin B6

An all-round vitamin, helping to maintain muscles in a good state, as well as being important to keeping your blood well balanced. Pyridoxine is found in good amounts in liver, yeast extract and whole grain cereals, as well as in eggs and milk.

Vitamin B12

Essential for healthy nerves. You can easily get sufficient if your vitamin diet contains liver, kidneys, eggs, lean meat. Vitamin B12 is used to treat one form of anaemia.

Folic acid

This is one of the group of B vitamins and is essential for the manufacture of protein and the production and repair of all the body cells. It is particularly important in maintaining a healthy blood supply and is used in the treatment of anaemia. It is found in fresh, green, leafy vegetables.

Lipoic acid

This vitamin helps to release energy from glucose and other sugars in your diet, so powering muscles for all your activities, work and play. So potent is this material that it is very unlikely that even a poor diet would contain too little, but in any case it is usually found with all the other B Vitamins.

6 · Sun and health

Ageing

As people get older the skin actually gets thinner; this is mostly due to a loss of the active elastic dermis, with its fibres of shape retention called collagen, and its rich supply of blood. We know, too, that the exposed areas, like the face and the hands, show a marked deterioration in the orderly patterning of the collagen fibres. Even the fibres themselves are frayed and bent and, in some cases, broken. However, the areas not usually exposed, say the insides of the thighs, show much less damage. What has happened?

The sun's ultraviolet rays have the property of being able to damage cellular components and thereby interfere with vital functions. For the elastic fibres to be maintained, they have to be constantly remade. This means not only a good supply of blood, but that there should be all the nutrients in the blood to feed the skin processes and, of course, to remove waste materials.

Excessive ultraviolet radiation will interfere with

this. The good news is that once the melanin pigment, the tanning, has been produced in sufficient quantities the effect of ultraviolet is minimized. So, the process of tanning itself is not ageing, it is the over-exposure before the body's defences have been mobilized that can prematurely age. Of course, ageing itself is a natural process, but it can be accelerated by excess sunning.

The Healing Power of the Sun

The soothing effect of the sun's rays comes from the longer waves in it, the infra-red, which are invisible to our eyes. These rays penetrate the skin to a depth of 6 to 25 mm and, because the energy in them is gentle, the warmth produced causes blood vessels to dilate, and so enrich the skin.

In medical practice, artificial infra-red rays, from lamps, are used to treat rheumatic conditions and soothe painful muscles. Indeed, infra-red radiation actually soothes nerves as well. Clearly, here the sun is of immense benefit, and you can feel it doing you good.

The ultraviolet rays in the sun actually kill harmful bacteria on your skin, as well as interacting with a chemical in your skin changing it into vitamin D. Consequently, ultraviolet lamps are used to treat cases of vitamin D deficiency – as in rickets – and also for certain skin infections. Obviously, your body needs sunshine, but not too much.

Because of the obvious benefits of infra-red and ultraviolet radiation in regulated amounts, there are lamps, and so-called sunbeds, which mimic the sun's light. Apart from their clear use in certain medical conditions, which of course can only be applied under expert supervision, ultraviolet-producing apparatus has been used for tanning without actually going into the sun. There are salons which provide such service; it is, however, important strictly to follow the instructions and to guard against over-exposure and *the eyes must always be protected* by using ultraviolet absorbing goggles.

If you are living in a country where there is little sunlight for much of the year, say Northern Europe, then such sources of ultraviolet radiation can be useful in keeping the amount of melanin in your skin at a healthy level to give a light, natural tanned look and to maintain a good level of vitamin D.

Sunbeds, however, can be abused, forcing a very deep, dark tan on European skin, which is not wise from an ageing point of view. However, if you are going to be suddenly exposed to strong sun, you can at least prepare your body for it. Unless some tan is already achieved, the harmful effects of excessive ultraviolet radiation cannot be escaped, except by keeping out of the sun altogether.

Clearly, the message here is that the right balance in tanning enhances health, and will retard ageing; too much ultraviolet exposure will lead to premature ageing, while no ultraviolet penetration will mean a vitamin D deficiency – unless of course you take vitamin D supplements. Remember that the wonderful feeling you get lying in the sun comes from the healing, soothing infra-red rays. The pleasure does not come from the ultraviolet, so you can use a high filter factor sun barrier against ultraviolet radiation without affecting your pleasure and enjoyment in the sun.

Eyes and the Sun

The sun does present a challenge to the eyes.

Your eyes will sparkle and the whites be bluish white if you don't strain them. Tears contain lysozyme which kills bacteria, so your eyes should be moist. Luckily, you have a reflex, an automatic reaction when something gets in your eyes – they water. Lysozyme to the rescue. But don't rub them too much. If something, anything, unusual happens (over-redness, styes and so on) always check with an eye specialist.

Never strain your eyes. So when reading or sewing cover your eyes gently every half hour with your cupped hands, and imagine *black* for three minutes. This is particularly important as a means of giving your eyes a rest from radiation. Today you can be in dilute European sunshine in the morning, and be carried by jet to tropical sunlight the same day. This is a sudden change, and your eyes need protection.

Eyes can adapt to higher levels of light, given

time, but sand and seawater reflect light and the levels can be too high for adaptation, so sunglasses should be used. However, here are two points to be observed. The first is that the sheer intensity of the visible light must be reduced and all sunglasses do this. But the other hazard for the eyes is the invisible radiation, the ultraviolet part of sunlight.

Ultraviolet rays enter the eye and impinge on the retina. The effect is as if the delicate cells there were being kicked. Providing the level is not too intense, the eye copes well, but the redness and soreness from exposure to the sun comes from too much ultraviolet radiation.

When there is glare, and that also means ultraviolet is present, the pupil contracts to reduce the energy hitting the retina. If then you put sunglasses on, the pupil dilates. Now if the sunglasses *do not absorb* the ultraviolet rays, they go into an unprotected eye. This is why some people get very bad headaches and pain in the eyes after a day on the beach wearing sunglasses without ultraviolet absorption. Make sure, and the drugstore or pharmacist will know, that the glasses you purchase are ultraviolet absorptive. This is essential for safe tanning.

Skin Cancers

The bad news is that excessive exposure to the sun can cause skin cancers. But this is not the same as saying that tanning leads to this. What is true is that lying in the sun, in a fixed position, without barrier creams, without careful preparation of the skin for the tanning process, without proper nutrition, is asking for trouble.

There are many kinds of skin cancers, and their incidence increases with exposure to strong sunlight. Fortunately, most can be cured entirely, by surgery, chemotherapy, or X-radiation, depending on the type, and depending on whether early diagnosis is made. Consequently, any change in your skin, particularly the appearance of spots or lesions coloured brown, black, red, white or blue should be investigated. The colours often change, and the spots can grow large and be very variegated in appearance. DO NOT wait for any spot to change or to 'go away', for though the chances are it is a non-malignant and easily treatable condition, if it is not, then modern medicine can be set in motion against it. Cure is usually no problem if the condition is caught early. Prevention is better than cure.

Safe tanning is important to guard against skin cancer. Do not expose any part of you that has wounds, cuts and other breakages in the skin. When the dermis has been cut through, the tissues beneath have no protection against harmful ultra-violet radiation. Clearly, when the dermis has been damaged, the wound, scratch, cut, abrasion, should be well covered by a suitable dressing, and not exposed to strong sunlight.

7 · Avoiding heat strokes

The human body must keep its temperature constant since the chemicals which activate our vital processes have precise heat tolerances as finely adjusted, as it were, as a quartz clock. Too much heat, and these materials begin to break down; too little heat, and there is insufficient energy for them to function.

Usually temperature is maintained by a variety of methods, depending on the circumstances, but lying under hot sun without any covering, as in nude bathing, or running about playing games on the beach, or out in the open under a hot sun, puts considerable stress on the body's temperature regulation.

When you lie without covering under a hot sun large amounts of radiant energy strike your skin and, irrespective of what kind of ultraviolet barrier cream you may be wearing, the infra-red rays, or heat rays, penetrate and are absorbed. This actually means that chemicals making up your vital processes become more agitated, as billions of them begin to vibrate and gyrate in your body cells, and your body temperature rises. The blood is the coolant of the body, absorbing heat from the tissues and carrying it to the skin. Heat is lost directly through the skin and through the evaporation of sweat from the skin's surface. If the surface of the skin becomes very hot from the sun and if you are wearing a lot of anti-perspirant then the effectiveness of the cooling process will be impaired. The conditions are then ideal for some serious over-heating to occur.

If you are running about, or engaged in heavy physical labour, or heavy physical play such as sex, then the heat generated from these activities compounds the problem, because there are then two sources of large amounts of heat, your own muscular work and the sun's rays. Again, the body's re-adjustment technique is to sweat.

Naturally, there is a limit to the amount of heat which can be siphoned out of the body by this means, and if the system is tested beyond its limits then heat stroke can occur. The immediate signs of this condition in its *extreme* form are that you feel irritable, and don't have much energy. Your thinking becomes confused, and you stop sweating – a sure sign that the body is overburdened. Coma then follows, and often the body temperature is found to be as high as 41.5°C. Medical personnel usually follow the same procedure in these cases as for *hyperpyrexia* or extreme fever: the victim is removed from the sun, stripped and cooled with water, or sometimes icepacks. Fanning is also used, as are cool, wet sheets. Injection of a saline solution is usually mandatory. Temperature is monitored because it must not be allowed to fall below about 38.9°C in the rectum; if treatment were continued past this point, body temperature would fall too far. When consciousness is regained, sweating is often induced by a drink of salt water.

Some victims of this extreme form of heat stroke have to convalesce in hospital, but with strong, fit people, recovery is fairly rapid. However, so severe is this form of heat stroke that it has the same kind of impact on the body as extensive surgery, and so a victim is usually monitored for some time, as there is always a danger of circulatory collapse.

Obviously the above is the result of severe heat exposure, but it can happen more readily as one grows older, or if one's diet has been very poor (too little salt, for example) or the body is fatigued. Extreme cases of heat stroke often occur on tropical beaches, but there are milder, less dangerous forms too. All are avoidable.

Heat Collapse

The blood pressure falls, the pulse slows down, and there is a short loss of consciousness. The skin is often clammy, and there is little urine to void. What has happened here is that the heat regulation mechanisms have been overwhelmed, with severe sweating at first. The victim feels giddy, and should rest out of the sun. When the patient regains consciousness recovery proceeds normally. Alcohol should be avoided, and drinks should be bland, like fruit drinks, or tea. There is usually a craving for salt.

Heat Exhaustion

Giddiness and weakness are symptoms of this condition too, but heat exhaustion occurs after a longer period of heat stress, as at the end of a month's holiday in the tropics, or when someone takes up physical activity which they can just about cope with, but persists with it beyond the limit. Usually, if age and constitutional weakness are not part of the problem, what has happened is that the body is gradually undermined, with its mechanisms being pushed a little further out of balance each day. The symptoms include insomnia, but the pulse rate is often unaffected, though the body temperature is significantly increased. Treatment includes a proper salt balanced diet, rest, and plenty of bland drinks.

Heat Cramps

When the body loses so much salt through the sweat that the nervous system cannot work properly (since nerves require sodium for their activity), muscles go into uncoordinated spasms, or cramps. This usually occurs in the legs and back, though sometimes the gut muscles are affected too, which may explain why in some forms of heat stroke vomiting is experienced. Cramp is accompanied by extreme pain. Before the pain, there is a period when the skin is pallid, and you feel very anxious.

Avoiding Heat Stroke

The prevention of all of these heat reactions is similar, namely high liquid intake, with alcohol in moderation, well-salted and seasoned nutritious food high in vitamin C, avoidance of extreme physical effort in the heat, and avoidance of being too long in the sun. Exposure of the human body to tropical noon sun is a severe shock, even for a few minutes. *Safe tanning, then, must really mean – keep out of the noonday sun.*

Sweating – Good or Bad?

Perspiring has a bad press. Countless millions of dollars are spent each year by major cosmetic companies to promote anti-perspirants. But the fact is, if you don't sweat you become ill very quickly, and will eventually die from your own toxins.

You lose water each day, and will be entirely unaware of it. About a litre of water passes from the body through the skin in the form of sweat. In addition to water, there is the protein waste (urea) which is excreted in the sweat and through the kidneys, as well as salts, mainly sodium chloride. There are a few other materials too, but in very small amounts.

Together with ridding the tissues of poisonous materials, sweating has another vital function, maintaining the body temperature at the correct level. As the sweat is produced by tiny glands in the skin, it is conducted to the surface through pores, where it evaporates, thereby cooling the body. When you are lying in the sun, large amounts of heat pass into your bones, muscles, blood and organs, which, if it were not ducted away, would lead to serious overheating, and eventual heat stroke in one or other of its forms.

There are two kinds of sweat glands on the body, numbering in total about two and a half million, with the eccrine type found in greatest abundance. These are located all over the body, but concentrated on the feet and on the hands. Through these, while sunbathing, you can lose up to three litres of fluid in a day, even more if you are physically active under the sun. The other kind of sweat gland, the apocrine, are concentrated around the genitalia, mouth, and eyelids, and the nipples and areola of the breasts. These respond to sexual excitement and fear, 'the smell of fear', for a person's distinctive aroma comes partially from the products of these glands. They are often closely placed near hairs.

Sweat, then, is an inoffensive and necessary product, and perspiring essential to safe sunbathing. Providing the body is washed regularly, there is no offensive odour; that only happens when bacteria start to decompose sweat. However, the pleasant aroma of some people, even four or five hours after a shower or a bath, comes from secretions from the sweat glands, allied with other odours from mouth and the private parts, which give them a marked power to attract the opposite sex. Though these odours are often, in fact, below the threshold of consciousness, and act subliminally, they are no less potent for that.

Anti-perspirants are of obvious use in controlling excessive sweating when the body is overheated, under the armpits, or on the soles of the feet. A deodorant, however, is useful for controlling odours that are unpleasant and which occur when sweat is trapped.

One of the healthy effects of sunbathing is to allow, with a gentle breeze, the body to perspire in a natural way, and that is one of the reasons why you feel so good after safe sunbathing; you have allowed your body to perspire as it was designed to do, with feet bare, and armpits unrestricted. However, to use a strong anti-perspirant over the whole body and then to go sunbathing, is at the very least to put yourself through stress, and a headache is the result along with, often, foul breath.

8 · *Topless and safe*

Most of the skin of the breasts is similar to that found on the rest of the body, except the nipples and the areola. The skin on the nipple is very thin, and very elastic. It is crinkled because, during cold, sexual excitement and breast feeding, the nipple increases in size, so stretching the skin out.

Because the skin of the nipple is so thin, and is unprotected by the horny dead layer found on ordinary body skin, it is very vulnerable to temperature changes, grazing, chapping, and sunburn. Furthermore, sunlight penetrates it easily, and the ultraviolet rays pass through very readily. In addition, there are virtually no melanin producing cells here, so the nipple itself cannot be tanned, though of course the areola and the rest of the breast can.

However, the breast is very different from other organs because it has no bone to produce its shape, and very little muscle. It is mostly made up of fat, milk glands, and small amounts of muscle fibres, not connected to any bones. It retains its shape by fluid pressure, the natural springiness of its tissues and the elasticity of the skin. Because there is so much glandular tissue and fat in the breast, it tends not to be as well supplied with blood as, say, muscles are, and this means that it is often colder than the rest of the body, and in hot sunlight can heat up differentially. Also the fatty tissue means nutrients are not so easily supplied, and consequently the skin of the breast will not tan as well as other parts of the body.

Men's nipples are similar in structure to those of women. Although they are so much smaller and often protected by hair, so exposure problems are not as acute, they require the same care during tanning.

If all these factors are added together, it might be thought it would be best not to try and tan the breast anyway. Certainly, women have protected their breasts against the sun for millenia, but does this mean one has to have those bikini marks after tanning? Not really, it merely means that safe tanning methods have to be used:

1. Use a barrier cream suitable for your skin.
2. Protect the nipple and the areola with a high barrier cream, first ensuring that these areas are moisturized with a good skin cream.
3. Do not lie in the sun with the nipples exposed for more than five minutes at a time, and leave a good half hour between each exposure.
4. Keep the number of exposures down to about five during the day, though at first it would be best to

proceed even more cautiously, exposing the breast no more than, say, ten minutes a day, in very short intervals.

With care, enough sunlight will penetrate the skin of the breasts to tan them gradually, and that is the purpose of safe tanning, an enriched colour without hazard.

The above tanning guide applies to moderate sun rather than high noon sun. I would suggest that breasts are never exposed to high noon sun unless you are running about, or swimming; and even that incidental exposure should be kept to a minimum.

The best way to tan the breasts safely is to expose them to ordinary dilute sunshine during swimming and games, or walking. This gives the body, over a period of weeks, time to produce the pigment of the tan, so no cells are likely to be damaged during the process.

If you have had your chest covered up for several months, and then go to a hot climate and expose the nipples and breasts even for half an hour on the first day, you are asking for some kind of trouble, since high noon sun can burn sensitive nipple tissue in this time or less.

What is often forgotten is that even when you are wearing a bikini top, or are covered with a towel, ultraviolet rays will penetrate the material, so care here is required too. You can also tan under a beach umbrella, because most of them let some light through, equivalent to the dilute sun of very early morning, or the sun in Northern latitudes during the spring and early summer.

To sum up, safe tanning of the breasts is possible, provided you heed the guidelines of low duration of exposure at all times, and no sudden exposure to hot sun without some protection. However, it must be remembered that individuals vary, and some people may have such sensitive nipples that it is simply best to forgo tanning the breasts altogether.

Care of the Breasts

Obviously, the more healthy the breasts are, the more safely they can be tanned. The chief problem with them is poor circulation, so I've included here some methods of improving the circulation since, as we have seen, safe tanning depends on a good supply of blood.

Hairs

Most women have hairs around the nipple, but if you are blonde they are often hard to see. Hairs can be removed by tweezers, but you need to do it a bit at a time over several days, rubbing in a germicidal cream to prevent sores which could so easily penetrate the breast to form an abscess. *Never* use a razor.

Washing

Use a mild, neutral soap. Ordinary soaps tend to dry the nipples too much. Use warm water, your fingers and hands for washing. Drying is particularly important, since the nipples get chapped. Use a soft to medium towel. If water or sweat gets trapped under the breasts, it can cause soreness and even infection. The nipples get clogged up with fatty secretions and so need washing with mild soap and running water.

Bras

Good bras – have no heavy metal catches
– do not cover all of the breast and are not too tight under the arms, so they do not impede circulation
– are made of thin material with pores to let the skin breathe
– are easily washed, and dry quickly.

Breast Form

There is no one particular shape which is the right shape. At about 16 to 18, the breasts are at their most upright, but they take on a more mature line quite naturally. The most common form has the largest amount of tissue above the nipple. Fluid, blood and lymph affect size. The amount of fluid is regulated by hormone levels and your general health. Correct levels are helped by exercise.

Your breasts are harder and less svelte when you eat a lot of animal fat, but softer and smoother if you eat vegetable fat. Oils *are* absorbed through the skin when you massage them in. Your skin gives breasts their lift, and so must be elastic and strong. So when you massage yourself, you help your breast shape.

Breast Exercises

Healthy breasts are warm and springy to the touch.

I give here a set of movements which break down the tensions of the day, and cramp in the muscles. They are methods for improving circulation to breast tissue.

These six exercises can be done every day, and are used to keep the tissues healthy and improve circulation of the blood to the breasts. You can do one each day, so you need never get bored. Study the illustrations carefully, noting posture of hands and feet. Approach each exercise calmly and gently. Go through the motions slowly at first, without effort. Exercise in a warm room either with nothing on, or a warm wrap, or on the beach. Never exercise in a draught or on a hard surface.

Good times to do these exercises are before going to bed, getting up, *after* a shower, or when you feel like it. They should be done without a bra. If you like, use a long thin towel, wrap it around the back up under the armpits, then cross over the chest so each bust is well supported by a 'hammock' of the towel *covering* it, and then the ends are tied round the neck.

At first, do the exercises in front of a mirror so you can see what they are doing to you. It is a good sign that blood supply has increased to your breasts if the nipples stick out.

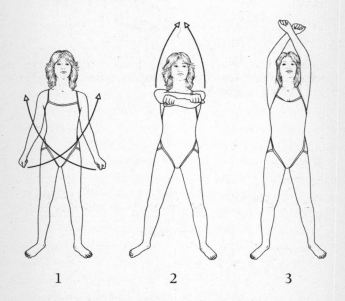

1   2   3

Exercise 1   Stand tall. Clench fists hard. (1) Swing arms up to shoulders. (2) Up on toes. Swing arms above head, then lower to starting position. Repeat sequence twenty times right arm over left, and twenty times left arm over right. (3)

1 2

Exercise 2 Kneel. Hands above head. (1) Press hands together, bring them down to bust level then raise above head. (2) Repeat eight times.

Exercise 3 Sit. Push inwards against knees keeping legs rigid for a count of three. Relax. Repeat twelve times.

Exercise 4 Press down upon knees for a count of three keeping legs rigid. Relax. Repeat ten times.

Exercise 5 Kneel. Clasp hands at the back of the head. Pressing gently against back of head, bring your elbows together and then open again. Repeat ten times.

Exercise 6 Bend and grasp ankles firmly. Keep arms straight. Push against ankles for a count of three. Relax. Repeat seven times.

9 · Massage

As previously explained, a good healthy tan depends on blood supply and skin health. Massage helps this and:

1. shapes your figure by moving excess fat by increasing circulation.
2. revitalizes the skin by direct stimulation.
3. pampers the body which makes you feel good.
4. improves muscle tone, making them springier, holding figure lines better.

You can massage in the shower, because water lets your hands flow freely over your skin and hot water helps to increase the blood flow, or you can massage with a moisturizing cream, so getting the bonus of improving skin sheen. Press as hard as you can without it being painful.

In one section I describe using a towel – this is very good because you rub off dead skin.

Topless Massage

With the flat palms of your hands, work from your waist upwards, to cup your hands over the nipples and sides of your breasts (1). Pass your hands upwards, over your breasts to your neck (3).

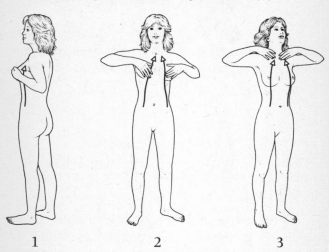

1   2   3

Arms

Direct the flow of water from the shower to cascade down your arms, and down the front of your body. Start at your wrist with the palm of your hand and move firmly along the forearm (4), over the elbow and down into the armpits (5). Repeat several times. Now do it to the other arm.

This is also very good for getting rid of the dead skin on the elbow.

4   5

Stomach

For getting a good firm tone on the tummy and just above the pubic arch, use the flat palms of both hands starting as in (6), working upwards over the belly button. Swap hands over (7) with a patting motion and continue.

Do this for at least a minute, with the water cascading on the tummy.

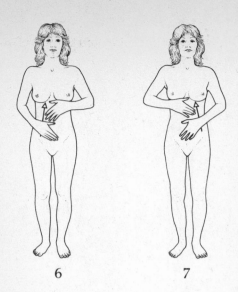

6   7

Thighs and waist

To obtain a good line from the thigh up to the waist,
start as shown in (8) and work up the thigh to the
waist, pressing quite hard with the flat of the hand.
Swap hands (9) with a patting motion and repeat.
Continue the same on the other side.

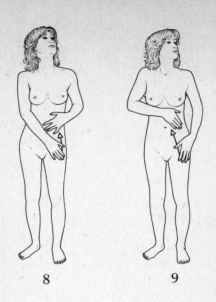

8   9

Thighs, Waist and Buttocks

With your palms on your thighs (10) bring them
over your tummy (11) up and round to the side,
over your hips to your waist (12); then sweep round
on to the buttocks (13) pressing very hard. Bring
your hands up over the buttocks to end at the waist
(14).

You should do this at least five times. It produces
very good smooth skin lines and guards against cellulite.

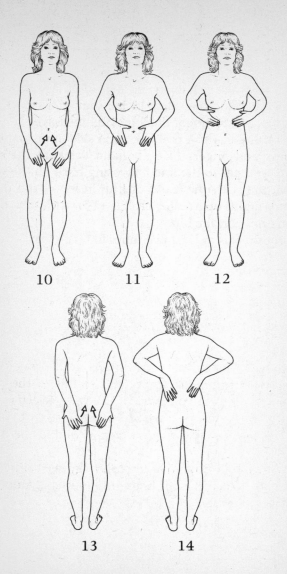

10   11   12

13   14

Legs

The legs are often neglected and this leads to varicose veins too early in life, but you can guard against this by doing the following massage.

Starting at (15), press on each side of the leg with palms and fingers of each hand drawing them up until you get to the knee. Pressing hard all the time, continue with the hand on the inside of the thigh, going right up to the crotch (16) with the other hand now on the hip.

Repeat this at least five times for each leg.

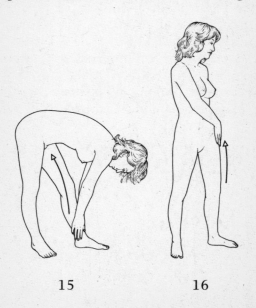

15   16

Towel Massage

This sequence shows you how, when you are drying yourself after a swim, shower or bath, you can use the towel with the invigorating figure-forming effects of massage.

Here the effect is rather different from using the shower as an aid to massage because this time you are working on invigorating the blood supply rather than smoothing the skin. The towel also gets rid of dead skin and produces a very good sheen.

Beginning with position (17), work upwards to the top of the thigh; then, by moving the towel from side to side, you can work on the thighs (18), buttocks (19) and waist (20).

Pull the towel quite hard from side to side, but not hard enough to burn the skin. Additional work can be done on the tummy by pressing hard in a circular movement around each side of the navel (21).

17

18

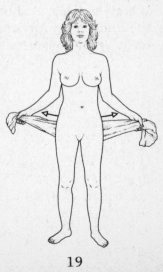

19

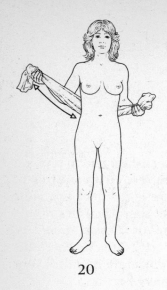

20

21

10 · Skin blemishes

There are many inherited blemishes, and many skin problems which can be completely corrected or at least helped these days. Here is a list of the more common ones. In general, all skin blemishes should be seen by a dermatologist. Also, none should be exposed to sunlight excessively. After a check-up, use a high filter sun screen preparation, unless your consultant physician says otherwise.

Acne

This is caused by bacteria irritating the pores. It comes and goes with most teenagers, but can be held in check by a healthy balanced diet containing fish and fresh vegetables, especially carrots and tomatoes. Stress often brings it on, so don't mope, get out and about, dance and run, swim and make friends. (See Eczema).

Allergies

These are real, inflamed reactions to foods, pollen, even jewellery and fabrics. What happens is this: your body is always on the look-out for germs, but is sometimes so active and enthusiastic that it mistakes harmless proteins and other materials for germs, and attacks them, thereby mobilizing defence mechanisms which, paradoxically, appear as rashes, itching, even watering of the eyes and nose.

If you find wool, say, or even silk or fur very irritating, you may have an allergy, so leave them out of your wardrobe. Some people have leather, even rubber allergies. The strange thing is that something you were allergic to a year ago, may be all right for you now.

The most common allergies are from food. Eggs, cheese, or other protein, and gluten (from wheat) are usually involved. So if you feel unwell or develop a rash when eating these foods, eat less of them or cut them out altogether. Look at food labels, because these allergens are in many processed foods these days.

Some people are allergic to the chemicals found in some sun screen preparations. However, preparations containing oxides of titanium can be used.

Birthmarks

These are usually strawberry or port-wine coloured, and are caused by swollen blood vessels. If they are small, just pick a foundation to hide them. If they are large, then a qualified beautician can make up a perfect foundation and cosmetic pack for you.

Blackheads

These are caused by fatty secretions from the sebaceous glands on your face choking the pores. Pour hot water into a bowl, cover your head with a towel and steam your face. You can then press out blackheads, but make sure you keep a clean piece of cloth or lint between your fingers and your skin. Then wash with mild soap, and rinse well. Dry with a soft, absolutely clean towel.

Many people re-infect themselves using a wet, dirty flannel. It is best not to use one at all, use your hands instead.

Eczema

This is often confused with acne, but here there is not necessarily an infection, often it is an allergy which extends beyond the pores. When washing, use only a freshly laundered towel, then put it aside for laundry. Some people are allergic to soap, especially with over-hot water. This causes skin peeling, dryness and rawness. If you scratch eczema areas, they can become infected.

In bad cases of acne and eczema, see a doctor, because you may need antibiotics.

Herpes

Herpes simplex causes cold sores, usually around the mouth, and is a virus infection. Many people carry the virus all their lives without developing symptoms until a patch of ill-health causes the sores and blisters to erupt. They go quickly. *Herpes zoster* is shingles and is caused by the same virus as chicken pox. It may lie dormant for many years and flare up as a painful inflammation of the nerves at a time when you are run down. So keep healthy, have fun, rest, play and eat well, to keep these at bay.

Moles

These vary in size from pin-heads to postage stamps, can be light or dark, raised or flat, with hairs or without. They often come in the teens. Usually they are of no importance, and can sometimes be beauty spots. If they are on your body, leave them alone, never cut or pinch them or make them bleed. On the face, if very worrisome, they can be removed very easily, but go to a dermatologist or a qualified plastic surgeon, never anyone else. Always seek medical advice if they become inflamed or begin to grow larger.

Warts

Warts are caused by a virus which is passed from person to person through contact. The virus causing them is still in your skin even when they disappear, and no one knows why they come and go. Most warts will go, if left alone, but you must never cut them, or make them bleed. Severe cases can be treated using surgery, chemicals, and/or cold-heat treatment, but never go to anyone other than a qualified skin specialist.

Psoriasis

Between two and four people per hundred have psoriasis, which is characterized by a dry, scaly, thickening of the skin. It can affect the nails, and most parts of the body. It is harmless, but can be unsightly. Although it comes and goes, it can often be controlled very well by various drugs, nutrients and ultraviolet radiation, though in every case, qualified medical supervision is essential. Sunlight is very beneficial in many cases. Cosmetics can cover affected areas when and where appropriate, but don't experiment, check with your doctor.

Howard & Maschler
O·N F·O·O·D

Elizabeth Jane Howard & Fay Maschler

'A joy to read, witty and shrewd'
Daily Mail

With wit, insight and an acute grasp of life's vicissitudes, Elizabeth Jane Howard and Fay Maschler, two well-known and prominent writers, have combined their culinary enthusiasm to produce a mouth-watering collection of recipes which are specially chosen to complement the varied occasions that life presents: A house-moving supper; a winter picnic; a seductive meal for a lover; dinner to enliven dull guests; food to cheer the abandoned man; a budget dinner party; a ladies' lunch.

For cooks of all levels of ability and lifestyle – those with limited resources, pressures of time, the rich, the put-upon, the eccentric – this is a stimulating, down-to-earth, inspiring cookbook which is as life-enhancing as the recipes are delicious.

'Two women with vast experience of family life behind them, celebrate both the strength of female friendship and the sustaining female world of food and comfort' *The Times*

0 7474 0196 9   COOKERY   £3.99

ROBYN WILSON

FISH

The complete A–Z of over a hundred irresistible fish and shellfish, covering everything you need to know about buying, preparing and cooking this most versatile and appetizing food – for beginner and expert alike.

FISH for your health
– Halve your chances of a heart attack
– Increase your resistance to arthritis, migraine headaches, multiple sclerosis, eczema, breast cancer and high blood pressure
– Increase your brain power

FISH for your figure
– Lose weight with low calorie fish
– Keep your skin supple, your eyes bright and your hair shiny
– Reduce the cholesterol level in your diet

FISH for your sex life
– Enhance your potency, fertility and libido

FISH – the ultimate guide to a new lifestyle of health and fitness.

0 7474 0037 7   NON-FICTION   £2.50

Mary Berry

BUFFETS

The perfect guide to buffets for all occasions

Preparing a buffet for a dozen people or more can be a daunting prospect. Everybody wonders what to make, how much to make and what is that magic ingredient which turns it into a meal to remember.

In BUFFETS, Mary Berry's practical advice, excellent menu suggestions and over 200 mouth watering recipes cover every possible occasion, providing invaluable help and encouragement to experienced and not-so-experienced cooks alike.

Including essential tips on planning and organization, hire of equipment, table decoration, presentation, garnishing and choice of drinks, the recipes are divided into such themes as, Finger Foods, Summer Buffets, Winter Buffets, Victorian Buffets, Scottish Highland Buffets, American Buffets, Italian Buffets and Indian Buffets. Each delicious section includes soups and starters, main courses, vegetables and salads, puddings, party breads and biscuits.

BUFFETS – the ideal companion to all help-yourself parties:

Also by Mary Berry in Sphere Books:

FAST CAKES
MORE FAST CAKES
FAST DESSERTS
FAST SUPPERS
FRUIT FARE

FAST STARTERS, SOUPS AND SALADS
FEED YOUR FAMILY THE HEALTHIER WAY
CHOCOLATE DELIGHTS

0 7221 1640 3   COOKERY   £3.99

A selection of bestsellers from SPHERE

FICTION

THE FIREBRAND	Marion Zimmer Bradley	£3.99 ☐
STARK	Ben Elton	£3.50 ☐
LORDS OF THE AIR	Graham Masterton	£3.99 ☐
THE PALACE	Paul Erdman	£3.50 ☐
KALEIDOSCOPE	Danielle Steel	£3.50 ☐

FILM AND TV TIE-IN

WILLOW	Wayland Drew	£2.99 ☐
BUSTER	Colin Shindler	£2.99 ☐
COMING TOGETHER	Alexandra Hine	£2.99 ☐
RUN FOR YOUR LIFE	Stuart Collins	£2.99 ☐
BLACK FOREST CLINIC	Peter Heim	£2.99 ☐

NON-FICTION

HOW TO GET A SAFE TAN	Dr Anthony Harris	£2.99 ☐
IN FOR A PENNY	Jonathan Mantle	£3.50 ☐
DETOUR	Cheryl Crane	£3.99 ☐
MARLON BRANDO	David Shipman	£3.50 ☐
MONTY: THE MAN BEHIND THE LEGEND	Nigel Hamilton	£3.99 ☐

All Sphere books are available at your local bookshop or newsagent, or can be ordered direct from the publisher. Just tick the titles you want and fill in the form below.

Name _____

Address _____

_____

Write to Sphere Books, Cash Sales Department, P.O. Box 11, Falmouth, Cornwall TR10 9EN

Please enclose a cheque or postal order to the value of the cover price plus:

UK: 60p for the first book, 25p for the second book and 15p for each additional book ordered to a maximum charge of £1.90.

OVERSEAS & EIRE: £1.25 for the first book, 75p for the second book and 28p for each subsequent title ordered.

BFPO: 60p for the first book, 25p for the second book plus 15p per copy for the next 7 books, thereafter 9p per book.

Sphere Books reserve the right to show new retail prices on covers which may differ from those previously advertised in the text elsewhere, and to increase postal rates in accordance with the P.O.

All Sphere Books are available at your bookshop or
newsagent, or can be ordered from the following address:
Sphere Books, Cash Sales Department, P.O. Box 11,
Falmouth, Cornwall TR10 9EN.

Please send cheque or postal order (no currency), and
allow 60p for postage and packing for the first book plus
25p for the second book and 15p for each additional book
ordered up to a maximum charge of £1.90 in U.K.

B.F.P.O. customers please allow 60p for the first book, 25p
for the second book plus 15p per copy for the next 7 books
thereafter 9p per book.

Overseas customers, including Eire, please allow £1.25 for
postage and packing for the first book, 75p for the second
book and 28p for each subsequent title ordered.